UNIPOL TOWER

UNIPOL TOWER
GROUP HEADQUARTERS MILAN

A PROJECT BY
MARIO CUCINELLA
ARCHITECTS

EDITED BY MANUEL ORAZI

New York · Paris · London · Milan

CONTENTS

UNIPOL TOWER
GROUP HEADQUARTERS MILAN

CARLO CIMBRI
Unipol Chairman

The idea of building a headquarters for Unipol Group in Gae Aulenti, within the significant urban development district of Portanuova in Milan, was born more than ten years ago. It was a time of great transformation for the Group, a pivotal moment marking the company's shift from being a medium-sized organization to a national insurance leader.

The acquisition of Premafin-Fondiaria-Sai, besides being the largest financial operation ever to take place in the Italian insurance industry, provided Unipol with a substantial real estate portfolio spread across the country. Much of this property needed to be optimized from scratch with efficient management criteria and new urban redevelopment projects, particularly in the Milanese area.

Among the acquired assets was a piece of land within the Gae Aulenti neighborhood, the only lot free from other properties and the management consortia, which were already operational for completed or near-completed construction.

However, the idea of constructing a building did not stem from the goal of merely carrying out a real estate operation by exploiting owned land in a crucial part of Milan's new urban dimension. Instead, it arose from a vision linked to the new prospective reality of Unipol Group and a strong communications drive concerning the spirit guiding the company. Therefore, it was not purely aesthetic architectural work, but a representative element of Unipol's identity, capable of encapsulating our way of being, our roots, and, at the same time, our natural inclination toward innovation. It reflected our way of working through strong relational networks and with an openness toward people, toward the city that is most imbued with modernity in our country. In short, we wanted to create a symbol of our essence that could express a distinctive leadership in the Italian financial market, also by means of the language of beauty.

These needs were conveyed during the briefings that preceded the project assignment, in a competition involving only Italian architectural firms, confirming our strongly national identity.

Among the proposals presented, all of which were extremely interesting with various perspectives and insights, the one by MCA – Mario Cucinella Architects won us over, not only for its alignment with our desired criteria, but also for its highly innovative technical value, and because it represented a "breakaway" from the surrounding spaces. This was achieved through a unique aesthetic vision in that context, characterized by a strongly iconic elliptical reticular structure that emphasizes light, transparency, and structural connections, making them the most powerful elements perceivable from both the outside and the inside.

At that point, we could have proceeded, as is done normally, by simply entrusting the execution of the project and all the construction phases to the expertise of specialists, behaving as cautious clients would but always waiting for a "turnkey" result. But that is not our way of doing things. Starting from the preliminary design phase with Mario Cucinella's studio, and subsequently during the actual construction, entrusted for the various executive areas to CMB and CEFLA, our role was almost that of a "self-contractor," through a body within Unipol's Real Estate Management that was ever-present in all the implementation phases, including the numerous structural modifications that occurred during the process. Always, of course, working in close collaboration with the architects and implementers.

For this reason, we can say that our Tower, the Unipol Tower – Group Headquarters Milan, was not purchased on the market, but rather was built by us with our efforts, day by day, detail by detail, alongside all the workers, and there are many, who constructed the building.

This book delves into the architectural, urban planning, aesthetic, and technological aspects (there is a lot of innovative technology in the Unipol Tower). From my side, I would like to return to the intangible and inspirational component of this splendid building, which we have chosen as the headquarters of the Unipol Group. I would like to stress how and through which words the Tower expresses our identity.

Six words spring to mind that, also via the Unipol Tower in Milan, evoke our way of being.

Time: The Tower, the group's headquarters, represents a step forward toward a new vision of leadership. A tower that embodies a time, that of contemporaneity, where spatial and temporal dimensions blend together harmoniously, rooted in the history of the company and in Italian history, but looking ahead.

Distinctiveness: The Unipol Tower is a highly characterized, distinctive symbol that allows us to present ourselves as something unique and concrete, without clashing with the city, but rather opening up to dialogue, giving it new space.

Complexity: Every architectural and engineering choice interprets and resolves complexity, transforming construction constraints into opportunities and new perspectives. A propensity to overcome the most challenging obstacles, made possible by the strong and diverse skills inherent in our DNA.

Harmony: The building's elliptical shape changes and transforms as it evolves upward. An inclusive form that relates beauty with sustainability, efficiency, and functionality in a balance that plays with spaces and creates a continuous exchange between interior and exterior.

Connection: In every detail, both macro and micro, lies our essence, our mindset. The texture that clads the tower, the intertwining of its structures, speaks of connections and exchange. The windows, the skin of the Tower, speak of lightness, welcoming and protecting, leaving space for the light that comes in and strikes from above.

Future: The Tower tells the story of our way of simply being "Unipol," presenting itself, changing the perspective with which one must look at tomorrow and act in the present.

I hope you enjoy reading this book.

UNIPOL TOWER
Group Headquarters Milan

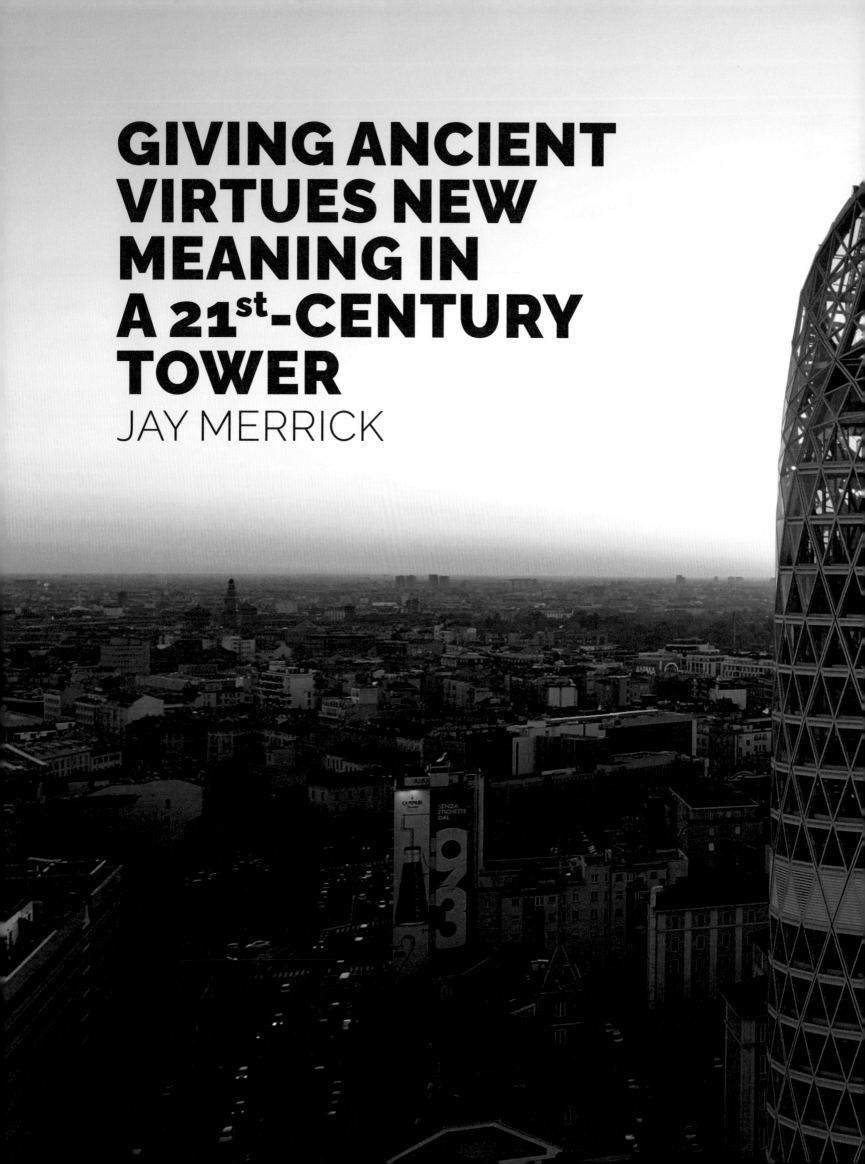

GIVING ANCIENT VIRTUES NEW MEANING IN A 21ˢᵗ-CENTURY TOWER

JAY MERRICK

For more than a century, the center of Milan has been a model, *par excellence*, of low and medium-rise architectural civility. Historic and modern buildings coexist urbanely in a city whose annual Salone del Mobile has become the world's unchallenged and epic feast of innovative design. In the last twenty years, Milan has gained two proto-epic hotspots of architectural verticality—the CityLife and Portanuova business districts, whose high-rise buildings have been designed by international "headline" architects including César Pelli, Zaha Hadid, and Daniel Libeskind.

The eminent Italian architect Mario Cucinella is among them, and his contribution to Portanuova is the Unipol Tower Group, whose elliptical plan and chrysalis-like form, sheathed in 2,200 glazed triangles, overlooks the vivid planar geometry of the Parco Biblioteca degli Alberi. The tower's design resists the usual marketing tick-box words—*stunning, landmark, iconic, unique*. This is "sensory architecture," Cucinella emphasizes, an environmentally responsive organism "much like a tree, with an orderly network of branches interacting with the surrounding light and air."

The tower is inherently bioclimatic, and at its physical and conceptual heart is an 18-story atrium facing southwest toward the historic core of Milan. It takes up one-third of the total volume of the building and from the office floors on the north side one can see beyond the city to the plain of Lombardy and the peaks of the Swiss Alps.

Passersby instantly see the tower's crisscrossing steel diagrid structure beneath the glazed outer envelope; on the south side, they glimpse the office levels and breakout spaces set back in wide curves around the atrium; they see the cantilevered entrance canopy flaring out "like a curling piece of bark at the base of a tree," as Cucinella puts it. And they see vegetation in the building's crown, a botanic garden and event space whose roof is angled at 60 degrees to maximize the building's height without contravening regulations about set-backs.

The internal environment is mediated by natural light and fresh, moving air in the atrium rather than being hermetically controlled by the building's state-of-the-art heating, cooling, and air-filtration systems. And this adroit balance of nature and technology has achieved a LEED Platinum energy-reduction accreditation.

Beyond its functionality as an office building, the design of the Unipol Tower responds to our collective environmental uncertainties, which could be summarized in two brutal facts: in 2020, the 1.2 trillion tons of pollutants in the world surpassed the entire weight of its biomass; and gas, oil, and carbon resources will be exhausted by 2050.

The tower's architecture is ambitious and original and belongs in the continuum of Milan's most interesting buildings over the last ninety years. The 1936 Montecatini Headquarters, for example, designed by Gio Ponti—architecture as "a crystal, a pure volume in which the city is reflected," as he put it. And, in the 1950s, legendary Milanese buildings such as Luigi Moretti's La Nave apartment block in Corso Italia, with its Expressionist-cum-Dadaesque angularity; BBPR's Torre Velasca, a Brutalist version of fifteenth-century Lombardian defensive towers; and, *primus inter pares*, the Pirelli tower by Ponti and Pier Luigi Nervi, Milan's most refined example of mid-century modernist architecture.

Mario Cucinella's deep interest in environmentally responsive design began when he was a student: "Climate and energy conservation were not a debate then. But I was always fascinated by the relationship between architecture and climate, and the shape of buildings in relationship to their environments. It's so fundamental."

His early environmentalist influences included Bernard Rudofsky's book, *Architecture Without Architects*; visits to hippyish environmental architecture in Arizona; the ecological design movement in Germany in the 1990s; and even the ventilation systems of nineteenth-century libraries and theaters in London.

In 2002, Cucinella began a series of journeys to different parts of the world to investigate historic relationships between vernacular architecture and different environments. This led to the practice's research-based School of Sustainability, and to a potent and rather poetic recent book, *The Future Is a Journey to the Past*.

Among Cucinella's many overtly environmentalist designs was the Emilia-Romagna Agency for the Environment in Ferrara—a building whose prominent cluster of ventilation chimneys recalled the wind-catcher towers he had seen in Hyderabad and Baghdad.

The atrium of the Unipol Tower is an inverted wind-catcher: instead of sucking air downward from the top of the building, it draws air through the glazed "curl of bark" at its base, into the continuous podium and atrium volume, and then to the top of the tower through the double-layer facade. The 230-foot-high atrium takes up one-third of the entire volume of the building, and it's impressive that Unipol Group welcomed a design that rejected the maximized floorplates typical of corporate architecture.

The moment one enters the building, the atrium and the massive diagrid structure that wraps around it dominate the scene. Nuts, bolts, and other connections are plainly visible. The triangulated grid of steel columns, each more than one and a half feet in diameter, curves away upward, holding the facade. The diagrid and the bridge structure that separates the foundations of the tower from an underground train line weighs 3,000 tons, the same as the building's internal structures.

The revealed form and details of the diagrid have an important effect: they convey a satisfying and even comforting sense of the dynamics of the structure; one can see exactly how it was built. The lower ten office floors are suspended from the columned structure of the floors above them, which are supported by perimeter trusses connecting the floor plates to the diagrid. This structural strategy means that the four-story volume of the ground floor reception space and podium level has only one visible supporting column—in other words, no visual clutter to interfere with the spatial drama of the atrium.

Fire prevention was a critically important issue, requiring 18 months of detailed discussions with fire control officials; one outcome is that the perimeter office windows are quardruple-glazed with one layer of intumescent magnetic coating; the cost of all the tower's glazing was about 40 percent of the total construction cost of €140 million (about $147 million).

Other state-of-the-art elements include a Wi-Fi network that can instantly report the exact positions of individuals in an emergency. This is a twenty-first-century inverted wind-catcher, after all.

The Unipol Tower's structural and technical innovations are one kind of narrative. But Cucinella's architecture is also part of another, more profound discourse that addresses questions that are difficult to answer in the twenty-first century. Do we have meaningful physical and emotional relationships with buildings and cities? Or do we think of them only as necessarily pragmatic scenographies that just happen to be ugly or interesting or chaotic? Do we question their fundamental relationships with nature and the ethics of coexistence?

Perhaps the Unipol Tower is a kind of chrysalis, after all—architecture as a point of transformation, a new kind of engagement. And does it also carry an echo from a passionate declaration made half a century ago? "The inferno of the living is not something that will be; if there is one, it is what is already here, the inferno where we live every day, that we form by being together," wrote Italo Calvino in his novel, *Invisible Cities*. "There are two ways to escape suffering it. The first is easy for many: accept the inferno and become such a part of it that you can no longer see it. The second is risky and demands constant vigilance and apprehension: seek and learn to recognize who and what, in the midst of inferno, are not inferno, then make them endure, give them space."

For over ten years **JAY MERRICK** was the architecture critic of *The Independent* in London, and he has also written architecture and art essays for periodicals and publishing houses like *Domus*, *Architects Journal*, *Architectural Review*, *Royal Academy*, and *Icon*. He has authored monographs on several architects, including Nicholas Grimshaw, Eric Parry, Schmidt Hammer Lassen, and Wilkinson Eyre.

AN AREA AIMING FOR PROGRESS
GILDA BOJARDI

A great spire, a wall of mirrors, a diamond, a wooden seed, a vertical forest, and a tall cylindrical mesh made of steel and glass are currently drawing the profile of Milan, a city that looks to tomorrow in an area that, albeit radically different, has always been effervescent, frenetic, creative, constructive, committed, fast.

The area close to Porta Garibaldi station that extends between Varesine and Isola is the very heart of the new management center of the capital of Lombardy, alongside, perhaps accidentally, what in that area represents the origin: the Pirellone and the Torre Branca, which rise up slightly farther away. The skyline that is being composed in the heart of the city is an exciting one: during the day it resembles reflecting ice, while at night it lights up like an amusement park. The more conservative-minded are critical, recalling a district made up of people, transportation, and work, but perhaps they are forgetting that historically this is a territory dedicated to progress, comings and goings, trade, business, travel, encounters, and even navigation. According to some, Isola got its name because at one time it was isolated: Porta Garibaldi freight yard to the south and Naviglio della Martesana to the east, what was once an artery for river transportation covered today by Via Melchiorre Gioia, excluded it from the rest of the city, and the only umbilical cord was a pedestrian walkway connecting Corso Como to Via Borsieri. It was a bustling area with families, workers (from the Breda, Pirelli, and Stigler factories located nearby), and artisans, where production took place in labs and workshops, and people lived in the overcrowded "case di ringhiera" (literally, railing houses). Essentially, just as is still being done today, with the difference that the spaces have changed together with the technological innovations that have breathed life into undulating high-rises and glimmering lights. In those days it was the manual skill, while today it's the intellectual, financial, and electronic skills that create local and global wealth.

Both duty and pleasure were and are located here. Farther up north, just beyond Via Melchiorre Gioia, opposite the newly built Unipol Tower, was the embankment that, after the Portanuova station was closed, remained in a state of abandon until 1973, when the Varesine amusement park was officially opened (actually, the merry-go-round operators had already been settled there for a few years). In rickety shape, it had a roller coaster, a toboggan slide, a tall observation wheel, not to mention goldfish prizes, fried food, and other amusements. Popular, carefree, and with simple dreams. The set for murder-mystery films and more serious ones, a site for organized crime gangs and illegal trafficking, it was the postcard of an unforgettable Milan. Our own Coney Island lasted until 1998, when the State railways decided to sell the area—a moment when, notwithstanding the red tape of bureaucracy, its metamorphosis began. In those days, nightlife was not known as the *movida*, but it wasn't at all different from today's: the new topography moved by a few hundred feet, to Piazza Gae Aulenti, a place where people can meet, without the merry-go-rounds, but with stores and cafés, where different and modern aspirations and illusions can be pursued. The amusement park lights can now be found in the Aviation Obstruction Lighting, the flashing lights signaling obstacles to flight, and in the LEDs that mark the facades of the high rises and create the atmosphere of a metropolis in the making.

      The area's commercial vocation remains strong and, as occurs in every mega urban agglomerate in the world, development is always aimed ever upward. But here the landscape is integrated with the green areas that give back to the earth what construction takes away. Indeed, the Parco Biblioteca degli Alberi, designed by Dutch landscape architects Petra Blaisse and Piet Oudolf, along with Studio Inside-Outside, rises here—a sort of large archive for flora that hosts 100 different species, 500 trees, and 135,000 plants. There is a unique context surrounding the Unipol Tower designed by Mario Cucinella, whose story is told in this book. An important piece of the Milan of the future, looking skyward, is immersed in nature.

GILDA BOJARDI, an undisputed figurehead of the culture of Italian design, since 1994 has been the director of *Interni*, a magazine focusing on interiors and contemporary design. In 1990, she conceived FuoriSalone, a design week held annually in Milan that organizes events and performances of international scope. In 2022, she was awarded an honorary Master's Degree in Interior and Spatial Design at Politecnico di Milano. She was the ambassador for Italian Design Day in Mexico City (2017), Madrid (2018 and 2019), Osaka (2023), and New York (2024).

A LAY CATHEDRAL

MANUEL ORAZI

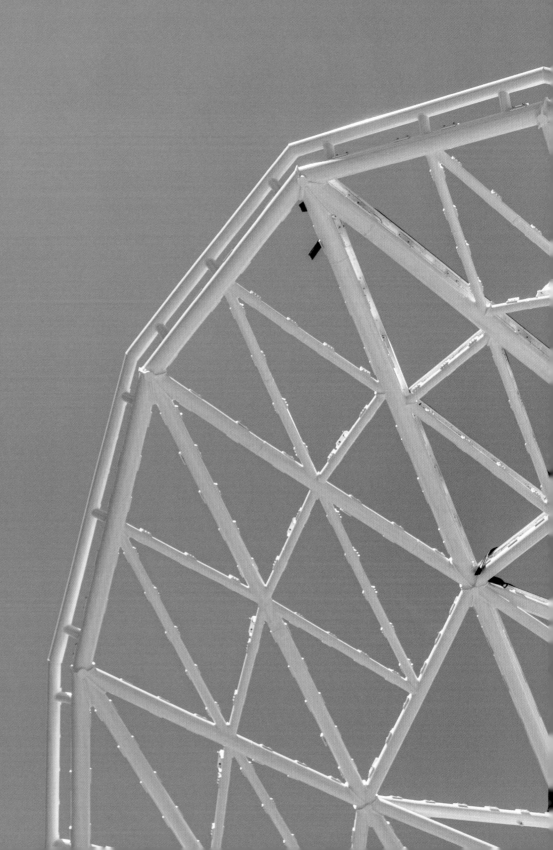

"Architecture is an abstract art. A work of art—that is, a work of architecture,
not just a structure—represents something different from what it concretely is.
It represents a thought."
GIO PONTI, *IN PRAISE OF ARCHITECTURE*[1]

Portanuova

In Milan, the period that stretches from winning the Expo tender to the advent of Covid-19, just slightly more than a decade, will be remembered as a second Belle Époque, a time of happiness where everything seemed possible.[2] Not just the work for the Expo, but also the activation of the high-speed train network, the decline in Rome's appeal, and a whole series of economic and social factors that favored this situation. Factors that are not entirely unprecedented, if it is true that in the history of modern Italy the cycles of its two major cities have always been antithetical.[3] In any case, the twentieth-century industrial triangle Turin–Milan–Genoa seems to have been overturned: in the new millennium the vertices of the productive triangle are Venice/Mestre–Milan–Bologna, and the distance between the capital of the Lombardy region and that of Emilia-Romagna has shrunk even more.[4]

The Unipol Tower in the capital of Lombardy adds a tangible sign to this recent change in the country, in a key point of the city not only and not so much because it is close to the central train station, but because it is in the Portanuova district, which, besides being close to another major train station, has become Milan's new hub of representation and self-representation.[5] Concentrated in this area of access to the city, steeped in memories linked to water (canals, basins, the *navigli*, the Isola district), are new towers, new master plans, old and new tertiary-quaternary activities that are unequaled in Italy. After all, in each of Italy's pivotal moments of modernization, there has always been a great insurance company. Suffice it to recall Piazza della Vittoria in Brescia (1929–32), where Marcello Piacentini deliberately involved the insurance companies at the time (Ina, Ras, and Generali) in addition to the new services (postal and telegraph office, hotels, tertiary sector) for the purpose of giving the piazza a more modern dimension of the city hosting it, i.e., a territorial dimension. Even though, in the case of Portanuova, there was not one single plan and the process of implementation was more elaborate and pluralistic—accumulating in the meantime were the Unicredit Tower (2011) by César Pelli, Bosco Verticale (2014) by Stefano Boeri Architetti, Casa della Memoria (2015) by Baukuh, Unicredit Pavilion (2015) by Michele De Lucchi, Diamond Tower BNP Paribas by Kohn Pedersen Fox Associates (2012), all situated around the Parco Biblioteca degli Alberi (2018) designed by the Dutch

architectural firm Inside-Outside—the Unipol Tower is an intervention that needs to be read from the broader point of view of the district where it is situated and that it has completed.

The Unipol Archipelago

In the decade that followed the merger between Unipol Assicurazioni, Milano Assicurazioni, and Premafin to become Fondiaria-Sai, which took place in 2013, Unipol Group invested a lot in Milan, acquiring various pieces of real estate, such as the headquarters on Corso di Porta Romana, Torre GalFa (1959) by Melchiorre Bega, the building on Via De Castilla, Hotel Milano Verticale, and, for a certain period of time, the Torre Velasca (1957) as well, the building that underpins Milan's modernity, a work by BBPR and described as "very Milanese" by Alvar Aalto back in the day. Unipol could have hosted its own offices in the Velasca, to settle, that is, inside an emblem of the city's *genius loci*, but it preferred instead to sell it to create a brand-new headquarters, the Tower in Portanuova, to give a clearer and more up-to-date sign of the financial group's evolution, and its renewed corporate setup. Unipol's presence in Milan is a metropolitan archipelago, made up of many buildings related to one another in different parts of the city, an archipelago that is still growing.

The Tower is the group's newest, largest, and most representative building, which publicly shows its renewed ambitions of international growth and no longer in Italy alone. No building typology other than the high-rise could have fulfilled this task better. Ever since it appeared in the US in the late nineteenth century, the high-rise has intrigued and awed the people and its workers because it subliminally reiterates the myth of the medieval cathedral, that is the "symbolic transfer of a rediscovered community"[6] that underlies its strength well beyond any financial justification, to the extent that, in its early years of life, it also conquered the Soviet Union.[7]

High-Rises

According to a study conducted by Professor Aldo Norsa, there are forty-three high-rises in Italy, eight of which are residential buildings, while another eight are public properties. The majority of them—more than twenty-one—are private, destined to the tertiary sector, and are located in Milan.[8] Besides the pioneering Torre Piacentini in Genoa (1940), all the others were built from the mid-1950s, with a considerable acceleration in the twenty-first century when, now that the self-made developers have waned, the client base has been increasingly expressed by international financial groups and favors renowned foreign architects: one example of this is CityLife, commissioned from Arata Isozaki, Zaha Hadid, and Daniel Libeskind.[9] If the epicenter of the high-rise in the twenty-first century has shifted to Dubai and to other Asian megalopolises, there has been a significant evolution in Europe as well.

In Europe, besides the Expressionist German projects evoking a "cathedral of the future" after World War I, the first real high-rises appeared in the 1950s, and everywhere they were mostly designed for office use, with the tendency to cluster together and be organized into "managerial hubs" like La Défense in Paris.[10] They are the symbol of modernization, and the tool to lower the incidence of the built-up area on the total area, but also to increase the value of the adjacent ones. They surpass the spires on the Duomo, the tips of the bell towers, to suddenly become, in both the larger and smaller cities, an important juncture in the urban structure, revolutionizing its pre-existing relations: the opening scenes of Michelangelo Antonioni's *La Notte* (1961) express for the first time the metropolitan angst of the inhabitant of the universe—Milan's management hub roughly coinciding with today's Portanuova district—which appears to be entirely artificial, in the implicit comparison with the historical city, that of memory. When high-rises are isolated, they can mark the entrance to a major city, like Brescia—the Brescia 2 management hub adjacent to the station—or in Bologna, where another Unipol Tower rises up at the city's southern exit. In the new millennium, London has been the city that, since the 1980s, has most renewed its skyline, becoming filled with high-rises of every kind, in particular a type of architecture that consumes less energy and is more concerned with its environmental side, inspired by the research of Norman Foster, Richard Rogers, and Renzo Piano.[11] Unipol Tower fits in with the latter line of research, for a number of reasons.

Architecture and Engineering

Unsurprisingly, one of the first architects of high-rises from the Chicago School, William Le Baron Jenney, had served as a military engineer during the Civil War. In the following century, the Empire State Building was completed, after twenty-one months of building work, in 1931. The construction of a high-rise, its builder said, requires the organization of the work and discipline, and it is the closest equivalent to war in time of peace.[12]

Mario Cucinella, who trained in the Paris firm of Renzo Piano, and Massimo Majowiecki, liaised like two generals in a multiethnic building site, organized in squads as though they were different battalions. The choice of leaving the structure made up of triangular modules is similar to the solution first put forward by Richard Buckminster Fuller and later optimized by Norman Foster aimed at building large-scale structures using a minimum of materials.[13] Besides its static resistance, the triangular framework has the advantage of leaving the structure visible, with none of the

finishings that in the past decades were, and still today are, applied. The legibility of the structure gives the project strength and substance, as Mies van der Rohe had already noted much before migrating to the United States: "Only skyscrapers under construction reveal their bold constructive thoughts, and then the impression made by their soaring skeletal frames is overwhelming. With the raising of the walls, this impression is completely destroyed; the constructive thought, the necessary basis for artistic form-giving, is annihilated and frequently smothered by a meaningless and trivial jumble of forms."[14]

According to Gio Ponti, Mies's great urban projects in Chicago represent the height of the marriage between engineering and architecture, because they are generated by prefabricated metal structures that are potentially endless and configured each time according to "a finite and not modifiable quality . . . Engineering creates prototypes, architecture creates monotypes."[15]

In the case of the Milanese Unipol Tower, the conversation between architecture and engineering, or, better still, its integrated planning, has produced an unprecedented monotype of a solid that is convex exteriorly and concave interiorly, with heterogenous anchoring to the ground, seeing the difference in height between the pedestrian podium with its entrance from Piazza Gae Aulenti and the accesses all along Via Fratelli Castiglioni, as well as the entrance at the corner with Via Melchiorre Gioia. The pre-established geometrical shape of the tower, determined by its structure, was modified and adapted in order to obtain the best possible architectural configuration. In other words, the ideal form became real or, to use Ponti's phrase, the prototype became the monotype.

The Structure

Cucinella and Majowiecki opted for a mesh-like structure made up of a grid of steel elements with a triangular frame, which creates an abstract motif. Although the exterior seems to resemble that of the high-rise on 30 St. Mary Axe and of Foster's City Hall in London, upon closer examination there are some important differences. Besides the different proportion determined by the entasis—the Milanese tower is much stockier than the one in London—in the upper part, the roof is cut diagonally; more importantly, it provides a large internal overlook without any supports, extending completely starting from the large atrium in the corner. This choice proved to be a structural challenge, in that to be able to support the entire building, after lengthy reflection, the interior had to be divided into two parts: the first seventeen floors are solidly connected to the exterior structure, while the following ones are suspended. Although the difference is not easily perceived, it is still substantial. This made it possible for the double view on every floor, overlooking both the exterior and the empty curvilinear void of the interior. In this sense, Majowiecki's experience with tensile structures matured over his long career proved invaluable.[16]

The Context

Every great architect brings with him the teaching and knowledge he received from his mentors, but also from his own colleagues and travel companions. Hence, the intellectual partnerships between Rogers and the Ove Arup firm, between Foster and Fuller, and between Piano and Jean Prouvé are just as important as the collaborations with Rogers, who as a young man was associated with Foster, Su Brumwell, and Wendy Cheesman—Team 4—while he subsequently became tied to Piano and Peter Rice.[17] The line of research of the latter architects, all of them pioneers in studies on economic and environmental sustainability through the use of technology on a large scale, has gone from being represented by a minority in the 1970s to being much more popular today. Indeed, Piano (1998), Foster (1999), and Rogers (2007) have all been awarded the Pritzker Prize.

In Cucinella's training, that of an architect who is a member of the following generation, besides his fundamental partnership with Piano, his encounter with Giancarlo De Carlo, someone who is apparently very distant from the milieu recalled above, was of vital importance. And yet De Carlo as well was born—by happy coincidence—in Genoa, like Piano, earning a degree in engineering in Milan before becoming an architect and a university professor in Venice. When, in the 1980s, he began teaching in the capital of Liguria, Cucinella was his student, and De Carlo was his thesis adviser. Piano, on the other hand, whom he had first met in 1968, was a privileged interlocutor who was often invited to the traveling school ILAUD.[18] De Carlo's attention to the context in every one of its dimensions (political, social, cultural, environmental) led him to become a precursor of sustainability, even though it is a term he never once used during his lifetime. One of his masterpieces, the Facoltà di Magistero (School of Education) in Urbino (1968–76), ends with a hanging garden overlooking the surrounding hillside landscape where, alongside the steel and glass volume cut diagonally and that provides light for the Aula Magna below it, there was meant to be café—currently it is a place where students can relax between classes. The analogy, a formal one as well, with the large panoramic greenhouse-garden at the end of the Unipol Tower is clear to see: this area will be dedicated to hosting public meetings and cultural events, thanks also to the café that will overlook both the exterior and the interior empty space. In De Carlo's own words, "An architectural work is authentic and significant when it is—as one would say today—a synergic

system where the meaning of each part lies only in the relationships it establishes with all the other parts, and the meaning of the whole of the parts lies only in the spatial and temporal relationships it establishes with the context where it is located."[19]

The Technology

Having to build a headquarters that can host around six hundred and fifty people, including workers and collaborators, the Unipol Group decided to organize a competition with its own internal jury in 2014, hence, just before Expo. Of the six participants in the competition, all of whom were Italian, unlike what had been the case for CityLife (ACPV Architects Antonio Citterio Patricia Viel, 5+1 Alfonso Femia Gianluca Peluffo, Matteo Thun & Partners, Enzo Eusebi + Partners, Piuarch), the project presented by MCA – Mario Cucinella Architects won. The building site began in 2019, just before Covid-19, with the excavation of a 32-foot hole, and it stopped for six months due to the pandemic, and then for another six months because of the difficulty finding the materials needed to build it. It was finished in 2023. Seeing the features of the area, closed in between two streets and Piazza Gae Aulenti, the building site had to be organized vertically because of the lack of space available—for instance, a climbing formwork was required, sky-tech more than high-tech. Of fundamental importance in this sense was the programming of supplies, as the lack of space prevented the accumulation of the materials, "just like in Manhattan," Cucinella stresses.[20] We should note that in countries where labor is more expensive—for instance, in the United States, the United Kingdom, and France—high-rises featuring a metal framework are prevalent because they can be assembled more quickly, especially when there are logistical limitations at the base of the site. In countries where labor is comparatively cheap—such as in the Persian Gulf (Dubai, Abu Dhabi, Qatar), India, and China—reinforced concrete frameworks prevail.[21]

The external shell of the tower has a double skin and has been designed as a dynamic system capable of thermally insulating the building in winter, while also limiting its overheating in summer. The geometry of the shell—a cylinder with an elliptical section—optimizes the facade surface, improving the tower's energy efficiency, as is the case of the ceilings, which are all radiating. The vast atrium as well guarantees temperature maintenance, protecting the southern facade from direct sunlight and favoring the natural ventilation of the internal spaces thanks to the "chimney effect." The awnings come with sensors allowing them to close automatically.

The specialized manpower companies are local—based in Emilia-Romagna (Cmb of Carpi, Cefla of Imola)—but the skilled workers are multiethnic, and they had to deal with the difficulty of a vertical building site, constituted by the welding of the external joints—a total of 1¼ miles—those of the structural mesh: the welding could not be interrupted, so teams and shifts had to be organized on the aerial worksite. There were no work-related accidents, and this was thanks to the efforts of the sub-contractors' division specializing in safety. Although this impacted the amount of time it took to do the work, it above all guaranteed worker safety.

MCA in Milan

During the design phase for the Tower, Cucinella began working in Milan more regularly, inaugurating a new headquarters in the city in September 2021; hence, the professional evolution of MCA is parallel to that of Unipol Group. Up until the present time, the buildings it has made in the city are, in chronological order, Green House Deloitte (2015), the new COIMA headquarters in Portanuova (2017)—next to the Unipol Tower—the San Raffaele Hospital Surgical and Urgent Care Center (2021), the Fondazione Luigi Rovati and the underground Museo d'Arte Etrusca (2022), not to mention the master plan underway for the Mind Milano Innovation District and SeiMilano areas.[22] What all these buildings have in common at a technical level is the growing use of BIM (Building Information Modeling), architectural design software that allows for a high degree of precision and can be used by the client as well, thus avoiding potential building site disputes, which is very useful after the implementation with a view to servicing. For this purpose, Cucinella has collaborated with Marco Imperadori.[23] In the transition from the enterprise to the labor, that is, from the design to the manual work, the construction process still remains artisanal because it is constantly being adapted to the circumstances found on site, such as the need for a vertical building site, the seamless welding, etc. As instead concerns the spatiality of the projects, BIM makes it easier to use curvilinear forms, which all of MCA's projects in Milan share. Nowadays, even prefabricated components don't necessarily have to be all the same and standardized; they can have different shapes and be cut with a 3D printer, so it is possible to imagine concave and convex spaces, planning from the start each individual component in stone, wood, or other material." In this sense, the work of the architect today can be more exploratory, less fixated with standards, guided, rather, by curiosity, instinct, and, why not, sentiments, as Antonio Damasio suggests, in search of different solutions never tried before."[24] Perhaps this explains why, although there are many precedents in the formal fluidity of design—from Eero Saarinen to Luciano Baldessari—the spatiality sought in the Unipol Tower and in other Milanese buildings is closer to the process of design, a research line that MCA has intensified in recent years—and the growing presence in Milan and in its events, like the Furniture Fair, cannot be seen as a random occurrence.

MANUEL ORAZI (b. 1974) works for the publishing house Quodlibet in Macerata, where he is the editor of several series of publications concerning architecture, the landscape, and urban design. After teaching at the Universities of Camerino, Bologna, and Ferrara, since 2020 he has been a professor at the Accademia di Architettura in Mendrisio, where he teaches the course "Città e territorio." He is a contributor to the daily newspaper *Il Foglio*, as well as *Domus*, *Log*, *Volume*, and *Urbano* magazines, among others. In 2021, he curated the *Carlo Aymonino. Fedeltà al tradimento* exhibition (catalog by Electa) at Triennale Milano.

[1] *In Praise of Architecture*, trans. by Giuseppina and Mario Salvadori (New York: F.W. Dodge Corporation, 1960), 217.

[2] Francesco Merlo, "Fragile e bella, è rinata Milano. Il primato ritrovato e il disastro di Roma," *la Repubblica*, October 29, 2015.

[3] Francesco Bartolini, *Rivali d'Italia: Roma e Milano dal Settecento a oggi* (Rome: Laterza, 2006).

[4] According to Istat, the geographic division in the northeast includes Emilia–Romagna, Friuli Venezia Giulia, Trentino–Alto Adige, and Veneto, cf. the study conducted by the Cgia of Mestre, www.cgiamestre.com/wp-content/uploads/2023/05/Nuovo-triangolo-industriale-6.5.2023-2.pdf.

[5] Luca Molinari and Kelly Russell Catella (eds.), *Milano Porta Nuova: L'Italia si alza* (Milan: Skira, 2015).

[6] Manfredo Tafuri, "The New Babylon: I 'giganti gialli' e il mito dell'americanismo," in *La sfera e il labirinto: Avanguardie e architettura da Piranesi agli anni '70* (Turin: Einaudi, 1980), 216.

[7] Jean-Louis Cohen, *Building a New New World: Amerikanizm in Russian Architecture* (New Haven–London: CCA/Yale University Press, 2020).

[8] Aldo Norsa, "Grattacieli in Italia: dal 1940, 43 oltre i 100 metri," *Il Giornale dell'Architettura*, June 20, 2023, ilgiornaledellarchitettura.com/2023/06/20/grattacieli-in-italia-dal-1940-43-oltre-i-100-metri

[9] Arata Isozaki and Andrea Maffei, *Torre Allianz Milano* (Milan: Electa, 2020).

[10] Pierre Chabard and Virginie Picon-Lefebvre (eds.), *La Défense, a Dictionary: Architecture, Politics, History, Territory* (Marseille: Parenthèses, 2013).

[11] Herbert Wright, *London High: A Guide to the Past, Present, and Future of London's Skyscrapers* (London: Lincoln, 2006).

[12] Carol Willis (ed.), *Building the Empire State Building* (New York: W.W. Norton and Co., 2007).

[13] Massimiliano Campi, *Norman Foster: Il disegno per la conoscenza di strutture complesse e di geometrie pure* (Rome: Kappa, 2002), 166–68.

[14] Ludwig Mies van der Rohe, *Gli scritti e le parole* (Turin: Einaudi, 2010), 3–4. Stanley Greenberg, *Architecture under Construction* (Chicago: University of Chicago Press, 2010).

[15] Ponti, *In Praise of Architecture*, 46–48.

[16] Roberto Masiero and David Zannoner, *Massimo Majowiecki: strutture* (Milan–Udine: Mimesis, 2015).

[17] Kenneth Powell, *Richard Rogers: Complete Works*, vol. I: 1961–88 (London: Phaidon, 1998).

[18] Renzo Piano, *Giornale di bordo: Autobiografia per progetti, 1966–2016* (Genoa–Florence: Fondazione Renzo Piano–Passigli, 2016), 388–89.

[19] Giancarlo De Carlo, *Nelle città del mondo* (Venice: Marsilio, 1995), 42.

[20] Alessandro Benetti, "Con Mario Cucinella nel cantiere della Torre Unipol, ormai quasi completata," *Domusweb*, September 4, 2023, www.domusweb.it/it/architettura/gallery/2023/09/04/con-mario-cucinella-nel-cantiere-della-torre-unipol-ormai-quasi-completata.html

[21] There are many variables that contribute to the choice of a structural system. For offices, steel is often used because it allows for more natural light filtering in. In any case, labor and its relative impact on cost is always a factor that determines the decision that is made, cf. Stefan Al, *Supertall: How the World's Tallest Buildings Are Reshaping Our Cities and Our Lives* (New York: W.W. Norton & Company, 2022).

[22] For all these projects see Anna Mainoli (ed.), *Building Green Futures: Mario Cucinella Architects* (Florence: Forma, 2020).

[23] Professor of Planning and Technological Innovation at Politecnico di Milano.

[24] Interview by Manuel Orazi with Mario Cucinella, September 7, 2023, cf. Antonio Damasio, *Lo strano ordine delle cose: La vita, i sentimenti e la creazione della cultura* (Milan: Adelphi, 2018).

A NEW MILANESE TOWER
MARIO CUCINELLA

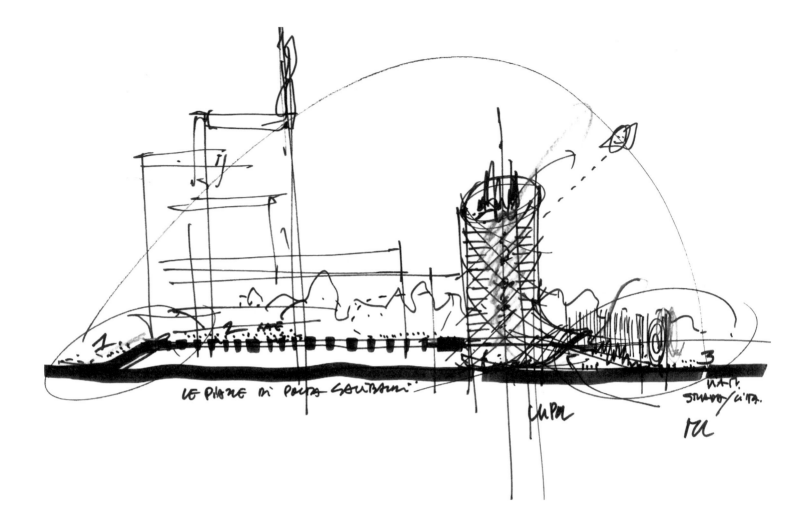

LE PIANE DI PORTA GARIBALDI

The project for the new Milanese headquarters of the Unipol Group springs from the juxtaposition of urban and environmental themes. The former are linked to the role of the Tower in the urban fabric of Portanuova and the city of Milan, while the latter are the result of an integration of climatic strategies that help define its unique form in the city.

During the competition phase, we developed various hypotheses expressed via different models that reveal the project's evolution. The final form is, therefore, not preordained; instead, it is the result of continuous adaptation not only to functional needs but also, and above all, to aesthetic ones.

The significant difference in elevation between the level of Piazza Gae Aulenti and that of Via Fratelli Castiglioni, along with the site's corner position, opened up the possibility of bringing the square into the large atrium. The Tower thus became the only building in the area with ground access at the city level. This led to a new square on the main street, where the building's skin creates a canopy covering a large part of it, thus marking its presence even at the pedestrian level along the external perimeter.

PRELIMINARY SKETCH OF
THE TOWER WITHIN THE
PROFILE OF THE CITY.

PLAN VIEW SKETCH OF
THE TOWER'S GROUND
CONNECTION.

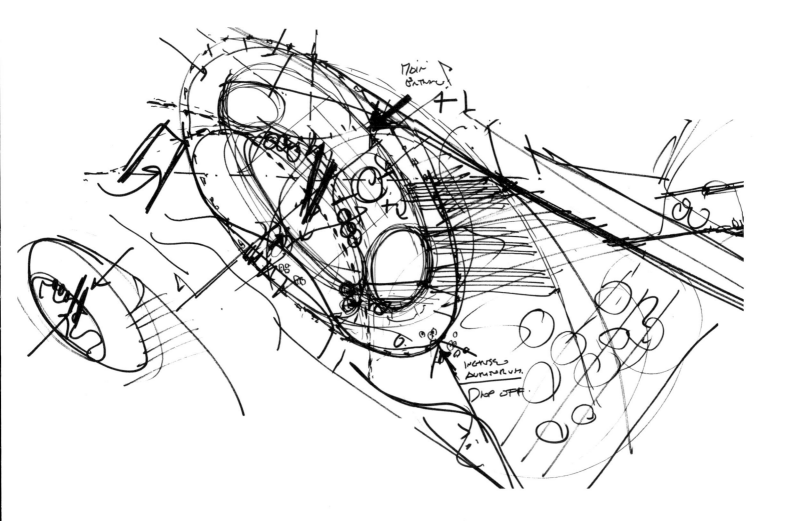

The idea of merging or connecting the building's atrium with the external square is one we also developed for the University Campus of Valle d'Aosta, which is by now close to completion. We can cite other architectural references where the relationship between atrium and square was fundamental; for example, the Guaranty Building by Louis Sullivan in Buffalo—considered, among other things, to be the first completed high-rise in history (1896), with a well-defined base, vertical development, and crowning—or the Lloyd's Building (1986) by Richard Rogers and Peter Rice in London, which was itself inspired by the Larkin Administration Building (1906) by Frank Lloyd Wright, also in Buffalo near Niagara Falls, unfortunately demolished in the 1950s.[1]

The integration of the atrium and square does not just have positive effects on expanding public space, especially in a metropolitan context where it is most needed; it has other benefits in terms of energy as well.

The large atrium, approximately 250 feet high, where the building's two entrances converge, also becomes a climate mitigator: thanks to its south-west exposure, this large void

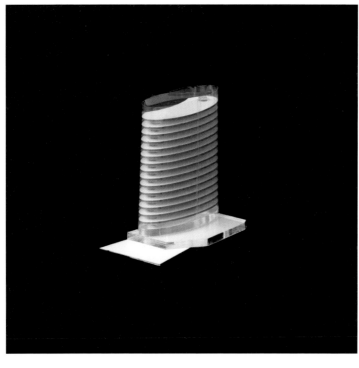
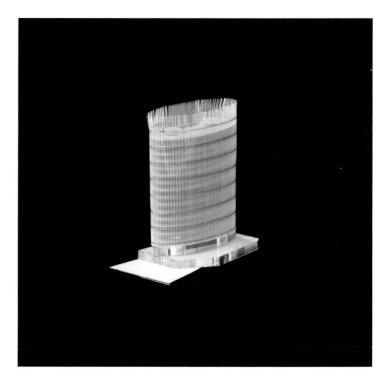
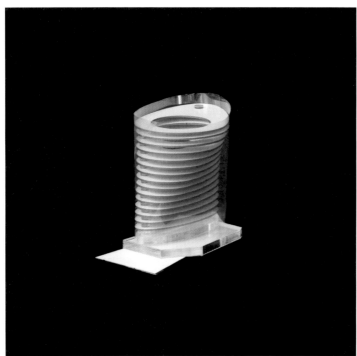
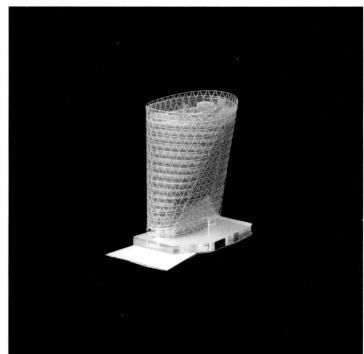

PHYSICAL MODELS
SHOWING THE STUDY
AND EVOLUTION OF
THE TOWER CONCEPT.

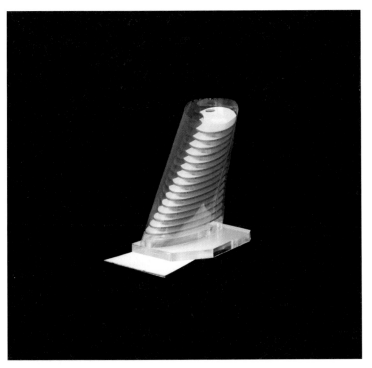
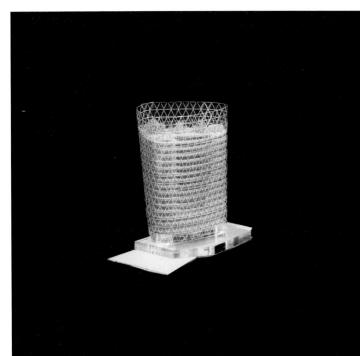

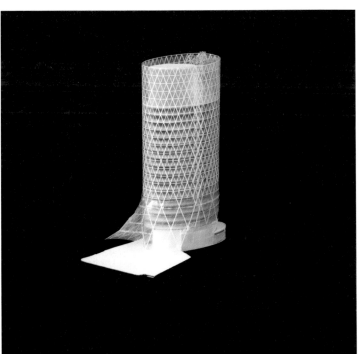
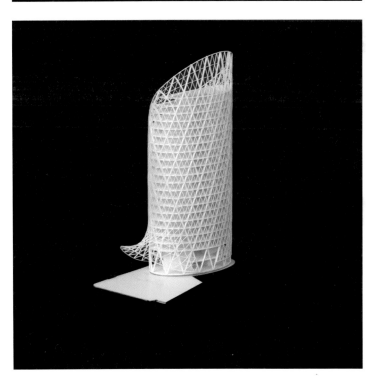

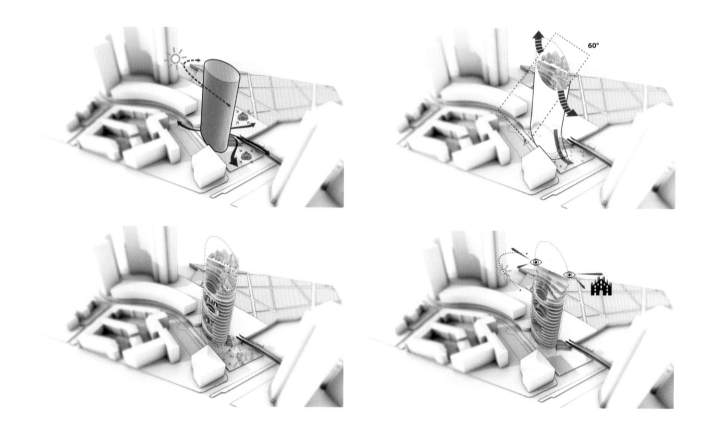

SEQUENCE OF CONCEPT
DIAGRAMS: THE
ENVIRONMENTAL AND
URBAN CONDITIONS
OF THE CONTEXT
CONTRIBUTED TO THE
FORMAL DEFINITION
OF THE TOWER.

PLAN (PRELIMINARY PHASE).

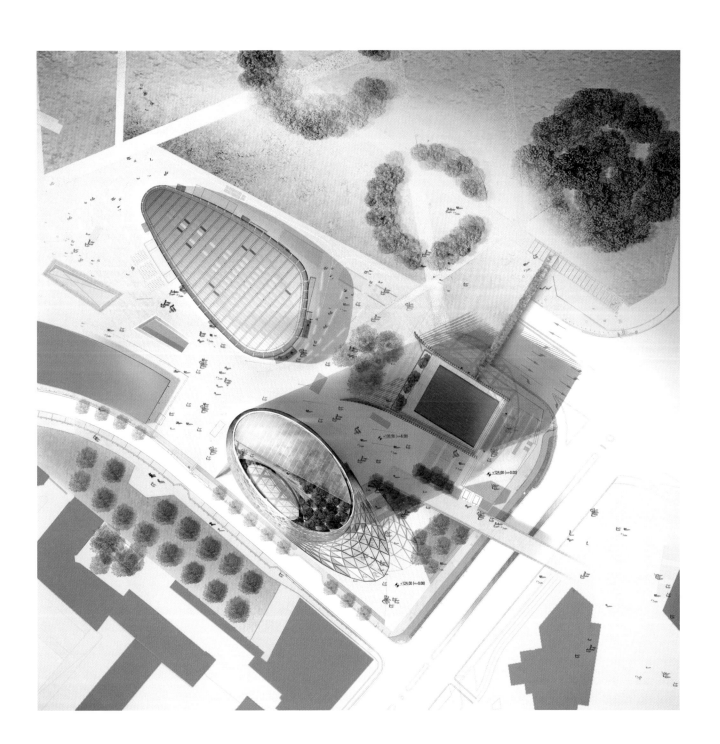

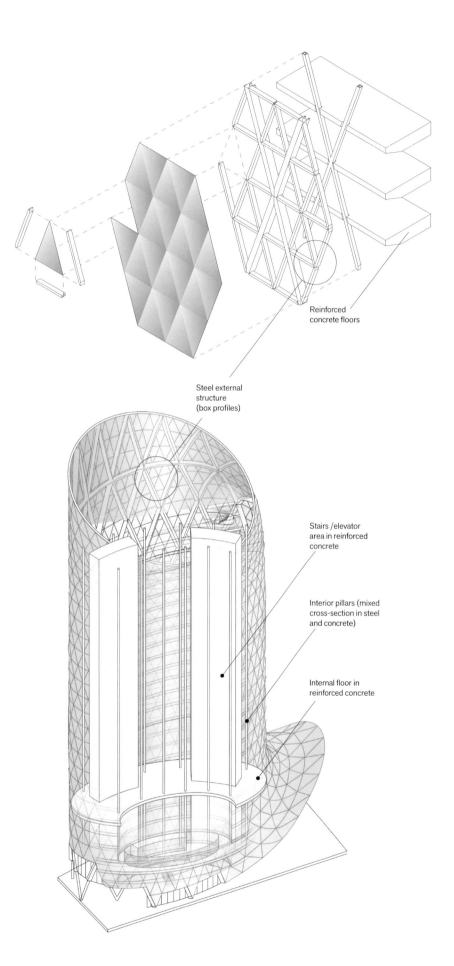

Reinforced
concrete floors

Steel external
structure
(box profiles)

Stairs /elevator
area in reinforced
concrete

Interior pillars (mixed
cross-section in steel
and concrete)

Internal floor in
reinforced concrete

ARCHITECTURAL DIAGRAM
OF THE TOWER AND DETAIL
OF THE FACADE.

FOLLOWING PAGE
AXONOMETRIC PROJECTION
OF THE BIOCLIMATIC
STRATEGIES FOR THE SUMMER
AND WINTER MONTHS.

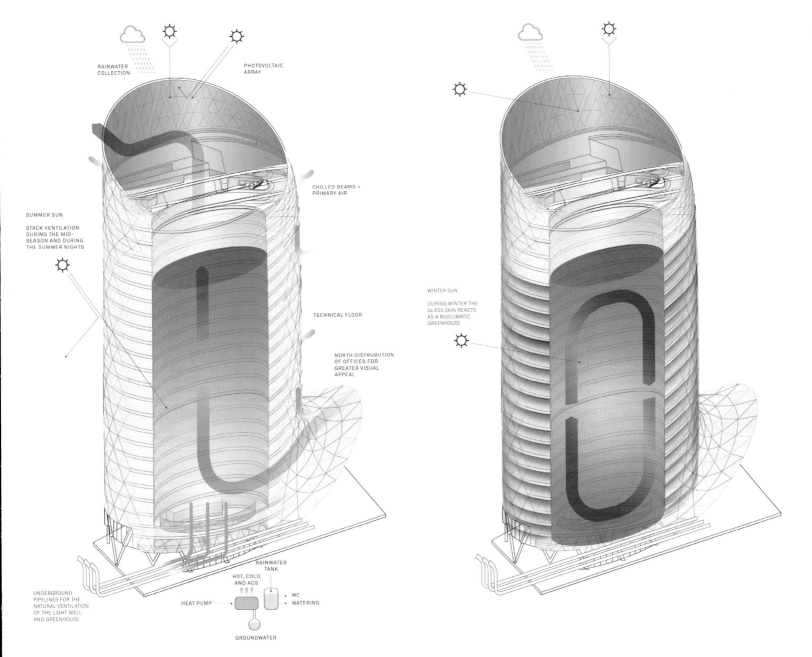

accumulates heat during winter, while promoting ventilation in summer. The use of the atrium as a space that naturally regulates the climate can clearly be seen in public buildings such as the British Library (1962–97) designed by Colin St. John Wilson in London,[2] or the Ford Foundation Center for Social Justice (1967) in New York, designed by Kevin Roche and John Dinkeloo, which, among other things, hosts thousands of tropical plants, acting as a large urban greenhouse.[3] This Milanese space, on the other hand, is an upside-down vertigo, as happens when one looks at mountains from valleys. The offices overlooking and encompassing this large void capture the building's vertical dimension.

Building a tower is always a gravity-defying feat. Just as a tree grows by overcoming a force opposed to its growth, the Tower for the Unipol Group headquarters, growing piece by piece, has overcome its gravitational challenge. Naturally, the effort to reach the top is the result of great teamwork, which allowed us to start from a simple, immaterial, and raw idea and, after a long design gestation, reach the point of laying the first stone. In other words, designing a tower means creating an organism capable of withstanding many external stresses, but also of housing miles of cables and systems within which energy, water, air, and data can flow.

The entire Tower rests on a floating foundation to allow for the crossing of the railway line. It is a great engineering feat that incorporates the experiences of the previous two centuries in steel construction. The building, with its metal framework, consists of 23 floors, some of which

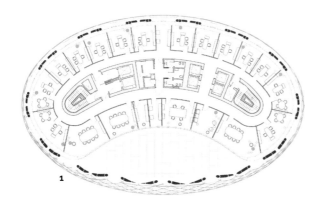 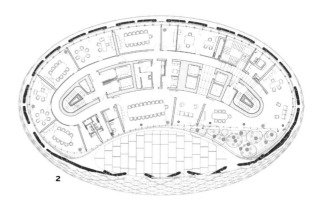

are anchored to the structure's nodes, while others are suspended. The supporting structure is made of tubular elements anchored to five-way nodes at various angles.

Over two thousand seven hundred glass triangles form the exterior facade, seamlessly adapting to the folds of the structure. Only from the inside can one truly perceive how each component of the building contributes to creating this effect; in fact, each individual element is designed and produced to give this Tower its uniqueness.

The Tower was designed using the BIM (Building Information Modeling) system, a method that allowed us to control a geometry whose complexity culminates at the building's top, cut at 60 degrees for urban planning reasons. This inclination generates a deformation effect in the geometry of the structure, which creates an elongation of the elements on one side and a compression on the other. The top is thus comparable to a large eye looking at the city, while thanks to artificial light it becomes a giant lantern at night. The top level, the apex of the gravitational effort, houses the greenhouse, a space where plants create a large winter garden with a unique view in every direction.

1–2. PLANS OF THE 18th FLOOR, LOCATED AFTER THE SKYLIGHT, AND THE 19th FLOOR, EXECUTIVE FLOORS WITH MEETING ROOMS AND OFFICES.

3. PLAN OF THE 22nd FLOOR, WITH A RESTAURANT, KITCHEN, AND PRIVATE ROOMS.
4. PLAN OF THE 23rd FLOOR, WITH A BIOCLIMATIC GREENHOUSE, CAFÉ, AND EVENT SPACE.

The Tower's geometry adapts to different functions: it covers the square, it empties out to create a large atrium, and the top is cut at a 60-degree angle, thus creating an additional covered plaza filled with plants from the greenhouse and served by a lounge. The structure has thus organically modified itself, transforming a repetitive geometry into an adaptive one. A new distinctive element in Milan's ever-developing skyline.

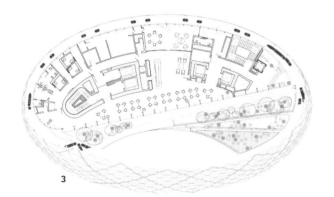
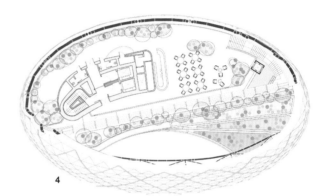

3 4

MARIO CUCINELLA was born in Palermo in 1960 and grew up in Campo Ligure, near Genoa, where he studied under Giancarlo De Carlo, graduating in 1987. He attended ILAUD (International Laboratory of Architecture and Urban Design) and worked in the Renzo Piano firm in Paris. In 1999, he moved to Bologna, where he founded Mario Cucinella Architects. After teaching at the Universities of Ferrara, Nottingham, Munich, and Naples, in 2015 he founded SOS (School of Sustainability) in Bologna. In 2018, he curated the Italian Pavilion (*Arcipelago Italia: Progetti per il futuro dei territori interni del Paese*) at the 16th International Architecture Biennale in Venice. His publications include *Creative Empathy* (Skira, 2016), *Building Green Futures* (edited by Anna Mainoli, Forma, 2020), and *Il futuro è un viaggio nel passato* (Quodlibet, 2022).

[1] As regards the Lloyd's project, "You could also see the influence of Frank Lloyd Wright's Larkin Building, in the juxtaposition of the service towers and the top-lit central atrium space, and of Louis Kahn's Richards Medical Research Laboratories." Richard Rogers with Richard Brown, *A Place for All People: Life, Architecture, and the Fair Society* (Edinburgh: Canongate, 2017), 177.
[2] Colin St. John Wilson, *The Design and Construction of the British Library* (London: British Library, 1998).
[3] Eeva-Liisa Pelkonen, *Kevin Roche: Architecture as Environment* (New Haven–London: Yale University Press, 2011).

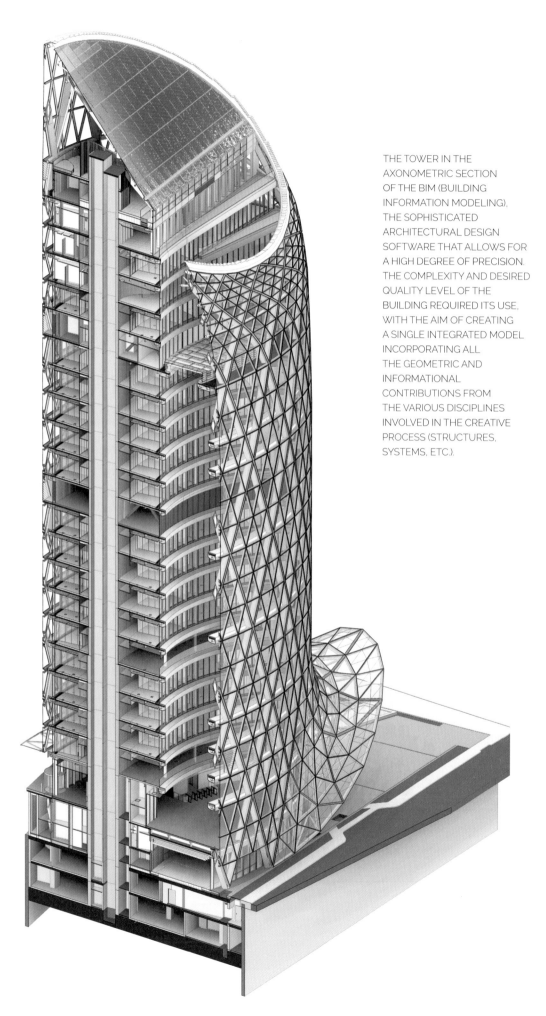

THE TOWER IN THE
AXONOMETRIC SECTION
OF THE BIM (BUILDING
INFORMATION MODELING),
THE SOPHISTICATED
ARCHITECTURAL DESIGN
SOFTWARE THAT ALLOWS FOR
A HIGH DEGREE OF PRECISION.
THE COMPLEXITY AND DESIRED
QUALITY LEVEL OF THE
BUILDING REQUIRED ITS USE,
WITH THE AIM OF CREATING
A SINGLE INTEGRATED MODEL
INCORPORATING ALL
THE GEOMETRIC AND
INFORMATIONAL
CONTRIBUTIONS FROM
THE VARIOUS DISCIPLINES
INVOLVED IN THE CREATIVE
PROCESS (STRUCTURES,
SYSTEMS, ETC.).

FOLLOWING PAGE
TOP, PRELIMINARY DRAWINGS
OF THE ELEVATIONS OF
THE TOWER.

CENTER, THREE-DIMENSIONAL
CONSTRUCTION DETAIL
OF THE FACADE.

BOTTOM, STUDY SKETCH
OF THE FACADE DIAGRID
STRUCTURE AND DETAILED
SKETCH OF THE FACADE.

Southwest View Southeast View South View

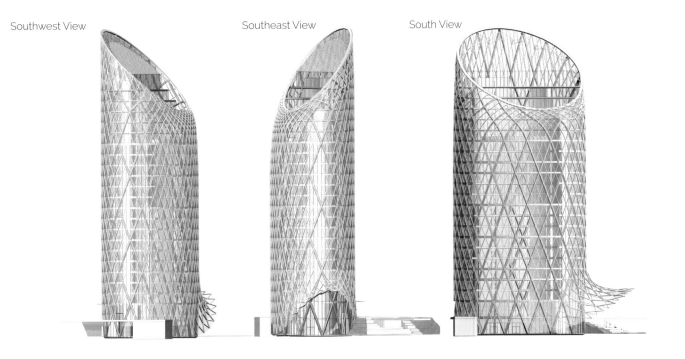

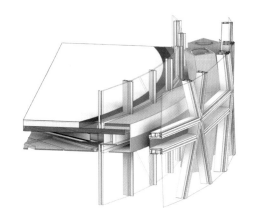

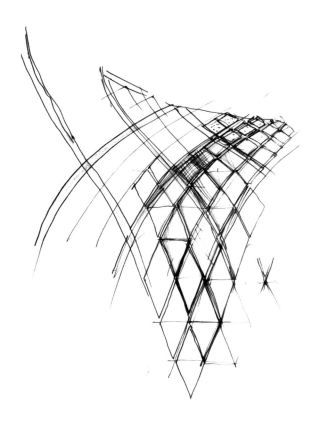

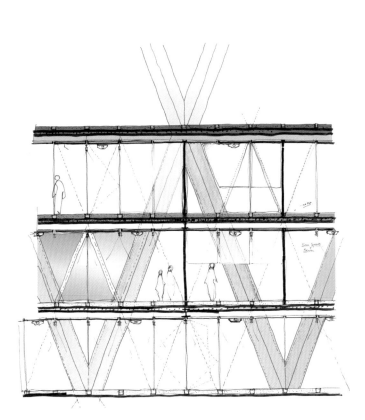

DETAILED SKETCH OF THE
BIOCLIMATIC GREENHOUSE.

FOLLOWING PAGE
DETAILED BIOCLIMATIC
SECTION OF THE
GREENHOUSE'S
FUNCTIONING IN THE
SUMMER AND WINTER
SEASONS.

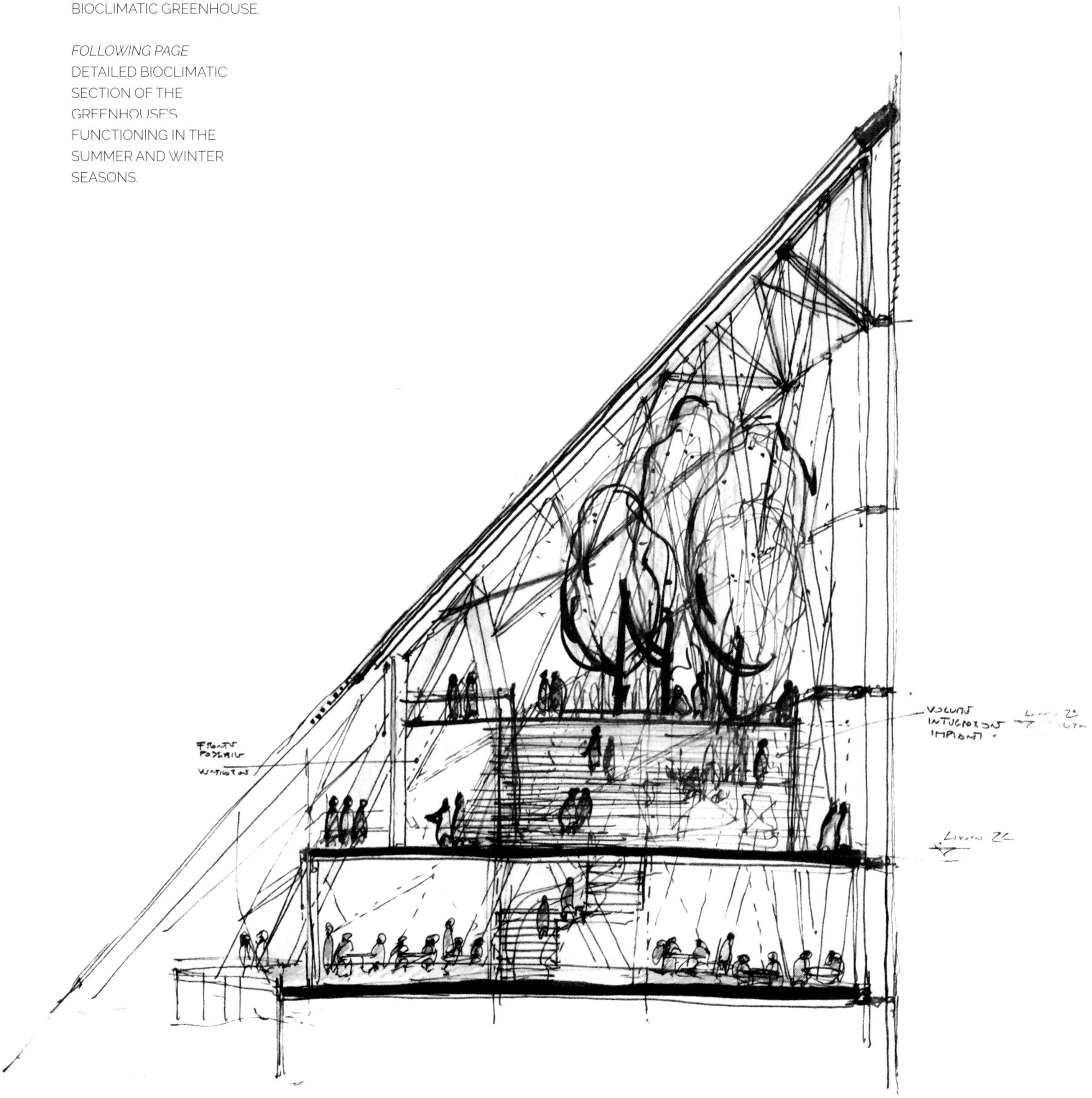

Summer Scenario_June 15th h 1:00 P.M.

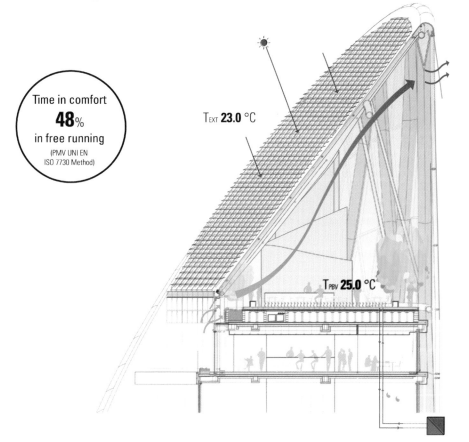

Time in comfort
48%
in free running
(PMV UNI EN
ISO 7730 Method)

T$_{EXT}$ **23.0** °C

T$_{PBV}$ **25.0** °C

10426.0 ▽ L A01
10246.0 ▽ L A02

10116.0 ▽ L23 B
10044.0 ▽ L23

9620.0 ▽ L22

 Winter Scenario_February 15th h 1:00 P.M.

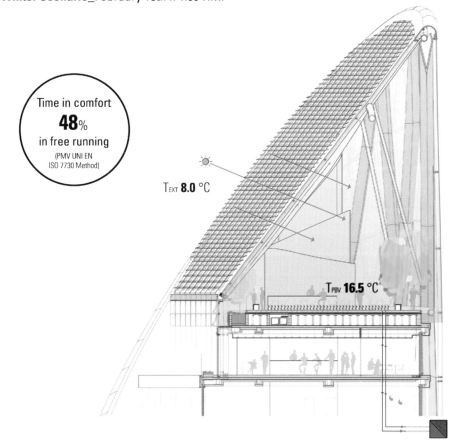

Time in comfort
48%
in free running
(PMV UNI EN
ISO 7730 Method)

T$_{EXT}$ **8.0** °C

T$_{PBV}$ **16.5** °C

10426.0 ▽ L A01
10246.0 ▽ L A02

10116.0 ▽ L23 B
10044.0 ▽ L23

9620.0 ▽ L22

ANALYZING THE STRUCTURE
MANUEL ORAZI
IN CONVERSATION WITH
MASSIMO MAJOWIECKI

To get to the headquarters of MJW Structures, Massimo Majowiecki's firm, you have to climb the hill overlooking Casalecchio di Reno, from where you can see all of Bologna and the unmistakable profile of the sanctuary of the Madonna di San Luca. Majowiecki is of cosmopolitan extraction and a war child: his father, a Polish soldier stationed in Italy and before that a student of veterinary science, and his mother, a native of Ravenna and a student of pharmacy, emigrated to Argentina at the end of World War II. After spending his childhood in Córdoba, Argentina, where he studied at the French La Salle boarding school, in 1962, after a long trip aboard the steamship *Federico Costa*, Majowiecki arrived in Genoa, where he was welcomed by his grandfather on his mother's side, Eugenio Bartolini, who accompanied him to Bologna so he could enroll at the School of Engineering. His parents would not join him until many years later. His polyglotism—at home the family spoke German, and still today Majowiecki has a slight Argentinian-Spanish accent—and his knowledge of several countries no doubt contributed to his training, as he himself explains: "My culture is differential, a technical term, because it is based on the valuation of one or more differences."

The School of Engineering of the University of Bologna was founded by Odone Belluzzi, the author of a treatise titled *Scienza delle costruzioni* in four volumes,[1] reprinted several times and translated into various languages. The distinguishing feature of this school consisted in the practice of intuitive physics, because before the advent of the computer, to be able to capture the soul of a construction you had to know how to use approximate calculation systems. Majowiecki earned his degree together with Belluzzi's students under the guidance of Piero Pozzati. He thus belongs to that middle-generation, between those who only used approximate calculation systems and those who, as is done today, only use a computer. Among other things, since 1967, CINECA (Interuniversity Consortium for Automatic Computing of Northeastern Italy) has been located in Casalecchio di Reno, where MJW Structures is headquartered as well.

To learn the first rudiments of electronic calculation, between 1968 and 1969, while he was writing his senior thesis, Majowiecki traveled to Sweden to meet with the pioneer in the discipline, David Jawerth, the creator, in 1962, of the roof for the Johanneshovs (now Hovet) ice-skating

THE FLOOR SUSPENSION SYSTEM CONNECTED TO THE STAIRWELL SHAFTS.

EXPANDED AXONOMETRIC DRAWING OF A SUSPENSION TRUSS AND VIEW OF THE INSTALLED HANGERS.

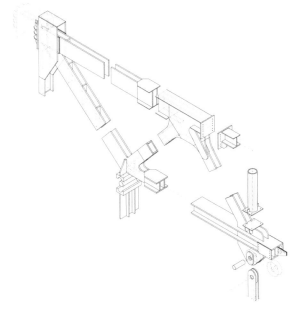

rink in Stockholm.[2] His interest in the computer evolution of calculus was equal to that in the light-weight structures imagined by Frei Otto,[3] from 1964 director of the Institut für Leichte Flächentrag-werke at the University of Stuttgart. The inclination toward this type of primarily metal structure created a distance from the days of his senior thesis between the Italian-Argentinian engineer and the Italian tradition of massive structures, where concrete has always played a predominant role: Pier Luigi Nervi, Riccardo Morandi, Silvano Zorzi, Sergio Musmeci, Franco Levi, just to mention some of the biggest names, are, in fact, all masters of reinforced concrete,[4] while the tradition of using metal structures is typically Franco-German.[5]

Majowiecki remarks as follows: "Having gone from planning that knew how to do a structural analysis even only intuitively or at an approximate level, designing arches, piers, or structural frameworks, in other words the form finding of the Modernist period, to today's, which instead seeks free-form design—pure geometry in the manner of Frank O. Gehry—is not a good thing. Believing that everything is possible with a PC often makes it harder to achieve a compromise between engineers and architects. Fortunately, this was not the case in the collaboration with Mario Cucinella, which was very positive, exactly as in the past when we worked together at the City of Bologna's Office of Unified Services."

Between 2006 and 2009 MJW Structures collaborated with Open Project on building the Unipol Tower in Bologna, which marks the entrance to the city from the southern plains, toward Romagna. As concerns the Unipol Tower in Milan instead, from the very start there was a serious problem with the foundations, so even before they could begin designing the actual building they had to intervene in its bedrock. As Majowiecki recalls: "We had a hole that was dug above the railway line; there was also the danger that the embankment along Via Melchiorre Gioia might collapse, which is why we conducted a huge amount of preliminary work that you can't see at all today. We decided to build a bridge with a span of about sixteen feet across the empty space over the railway, adding piles over two hundred feet deep to reinforce the ground, specifically to prevent the tower from interacting with the structures of the railway line and thus avoid any potential short-circuiting of the latter."

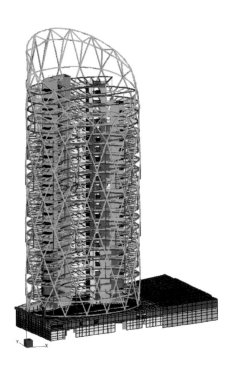

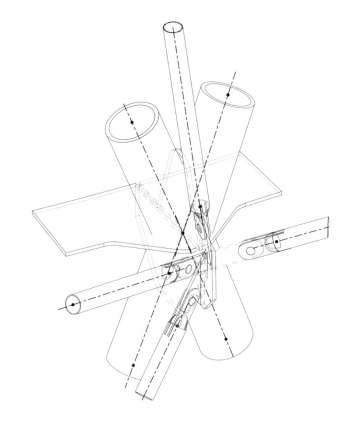

Added to the complexity of the topography of the foundation was the change in the materials: from the concrete of the base to the metal structure of the elevation. After consulting with Mario Cucinella Architects, a system typologically known as diagrid was chosen for the tower,[6] "one of the most interesting for elevated buildings because, while we usually solely use the stairwell as a large spinal column supporting all the floors of the high-rise, the Unipol Tower also relies partly on external load-bearing, increasing static efficiency."

Cucinella can be attributed the opening of the interior space, the large and curvilinear balconies overlooking the two entrances—the one lower down, at the corner between Via Melchiorre Gioia and Via Fratelli Castiglioni, and the one at the level of Piazza Gae Aulenti—an opening that the diagrid allows for: "This is no doubt an architectural choice. The absence of pillars or tie rods affords lightness and airiness, and you can't even feel the change from the seventeenth floor upward, that is, the fact that up to the twenty-third floor the two elevator shafts serve as anchoring systems for the ones below; in other words, going up what previously was compressed now becomes suspended, the object of 'appension,' as we refer to it."

Usually, the main danger for high-rises is the wind, more than the possibility of earthquakes occurring. This is why tube-in-tube systems are often used,[7] as they are already wind-resistant. But for the Unipol Tower in Milan, we chose the diagrid. Although it is generally used for towers over 650 feet tall, the complexity of the foundation—as we said before, over the railway line—suggested that we use it in this case as well, so that the facades could collaborate with the building's overall stability. Furthermore, special attention was paid to the aerodynamic study of the tower, meticulously documented in an in-depth article on the subject:[8] "This is more or less a theoretical study, because the tower is really not so tall. Of course, it is over 390 feet tall, but there are some

PERSPECTIVE VIEW OF THE
TOWER'S LOAD CALCULATION
MODEL, EXCLUDING LOAD
AREAS, WITH RIGID FLOOR   SCHEMATIC VIEW OF THE
LINKS ON THE RIGHT.   SUSPENSION IN THE LOAD
                              CALCULATION MODEL.

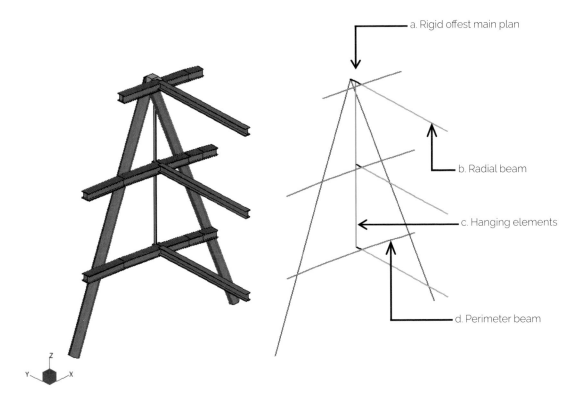

a. Rigid offest main plan

b. Radial beam

c. Hanging elements

d. Perimeter beam

much taller ones located in the same area. For wind-resistance, the macroeffect is undeniable, there are no problems with the structure, but you have to be careful about the microeffects, that is, about what happens at a local level, especially on the facade, even though the aerodynamic shape does help. For this reason as well, there is a specific diagrid for the facade." Majowiecki is also an expert on membranes and tensile structures with a support function. As he has often said on the matter: "The only substantial difference is whether the membranes are placed in a horizontal or a vertical position, because even though the stresses change, they're still membranes. In the Unipol Tower in Milan, the verticality makes the transmission of forces in the intersections of the mesh, that is, in the metal joints, relevant. This is a fundamental structural element, similar to what we find in a necklace: all it takes is for one element to break to create serious damage to all the rest. So it is crucial that every joint should have the proper rigidity, as it is there that the whole strain is channeled, particularly in the joints located lower down—the farther down you go the greater the strains—which, because of this, must be studied and monitored more closely."

Massimo Majowiecki has two firms: the first of these, which is smaller, is located in a bucolic setting, at the top of a hill, dedicated solely to structural conception; the other, instead, with over fifty employees, is located farther down, right in Bologna, and is devoted to project execution. The difference between them is roughly the difference that existed between Athens and Sparta.

MJW is renowned for having designed several tensile structures for important public buildings, from the spoke-wheel roof of the Olympic Stadium in Rome[9] to the entire Delle Alpi Stadium in Turin, both built for the 1990 FIFA World Cup. His signature is also on the Juventus Stadium/Allianz Stadium, 2011, rising up on the ruins of the Delle Alpi, a one-of-a-kind example of an architect being commissioned to rebuild one of his own works, not because of structural

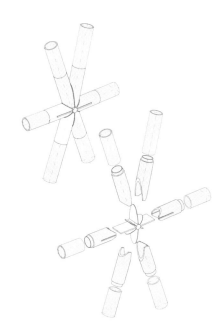

issues but in order to fulfill the new managerial and logistical demands of soccer. Besides stadiums, MJW previously designed sports stadium roofs in Ravenna, Pesaro, Athens, and Montreal, and has collaborated on the structural design of other buildings with some of the most famous architectural firms in Italy and abroad: the Nuvola by Massimiliano and Doriana Fuksas at the EUR and the Stazione Tiburtina by ABDR Architetti Associati, both in Rome; Torre Sanpaolo by Renzo Piano in Turin; Braga Stadium in Portugal, a project by Eduardo Souto de Moura; Pavilion of Islamic Arts designed by Mario Bellini and Rudy Ricciotti at the Louvre Museum in Paris; not to mention the most recent major projects in Kazakhstan, Cameroon, and Egypt. In short, when it comes to quantity and variety of work, Massimo Majowiecki is definitely one of the greatest structural engineers today, and has been for the past fifty years.

MASSIMO MAJOWIECKI (1945) is an engineer and architect specializing in the design of large roofs and tensile structures. Of Polish origin, he was educated at the University of Bologna. He worked as a consulting architect on the construction of the Stadio delle Alpi and the Allianz Stadium in Turin, as well as designing the roof for the Olympic Stadium in Rome. He was also the structural engineer for EUR's Nuovo Centro Congressi in Rome, signed by Massimiliano Fuksas, and for the roof of the Department of Islamic Arts at the Louvre, designed by architects Mario Bellini and Rudy Ricciotti.

[1] Odone Belluzzi, *Scienza delle costruzioni*, 4 vols. (Bologna: Zanichelli, 1955).
[2] Roberto Masiero and David Zannoner, *Massimo Majowiecki: Strutture* (Milan–Udine: Mimesis, 2015), 45.
[3] Frei Otto, *Das hängende Dach: Gestalt und Struktur* (Berlin: Bauwelt, 1954).
[4] Tullia Iori and Alessandro Marzo Magno, *150 anni di storia del cemento in Italia, 1861–2011: Le opere, gli uomini, le imprese* (Rome: Gangemi, 2011).

[5] Sigfried Giedion, *Building in France, Building in Iron, Building in Ferroconcrete* (Los Angeles: The Getty Center for the History of Art, 1995).
[6] A framework (diagonal grid) with a triangular or rhomboid geometry used in the construction of a building or around its perimeter, which allows for the use of less structural material with clear advantages in terms of energetic sustainability. Cf. Terri Meyer Boake, *Diagrid Structures:*

Systems, Connections, Details (Basel: Birkhauser, 2014).
[7] Cf. Heino Engel, *Atlante delle strutture* (Turin: Utet, 2001).
[8] Massimo Majowiecki and Giovanni Berti, "La nuova torre Unipol di Milano," *Costruzioni metalliche* 4 (2023), 11–25.
[9] Massimo Majowiecki, *The New Suspended Roof for the Olympic Stadium in Rome*, IASS International Congress, Copenhagen, August 1991.

AXONOMETRIC VIEW OF THE TECHNICAL STRUCTURAL DESIGN MODEL USING FEM (FINITE ELEMENT METHOD).

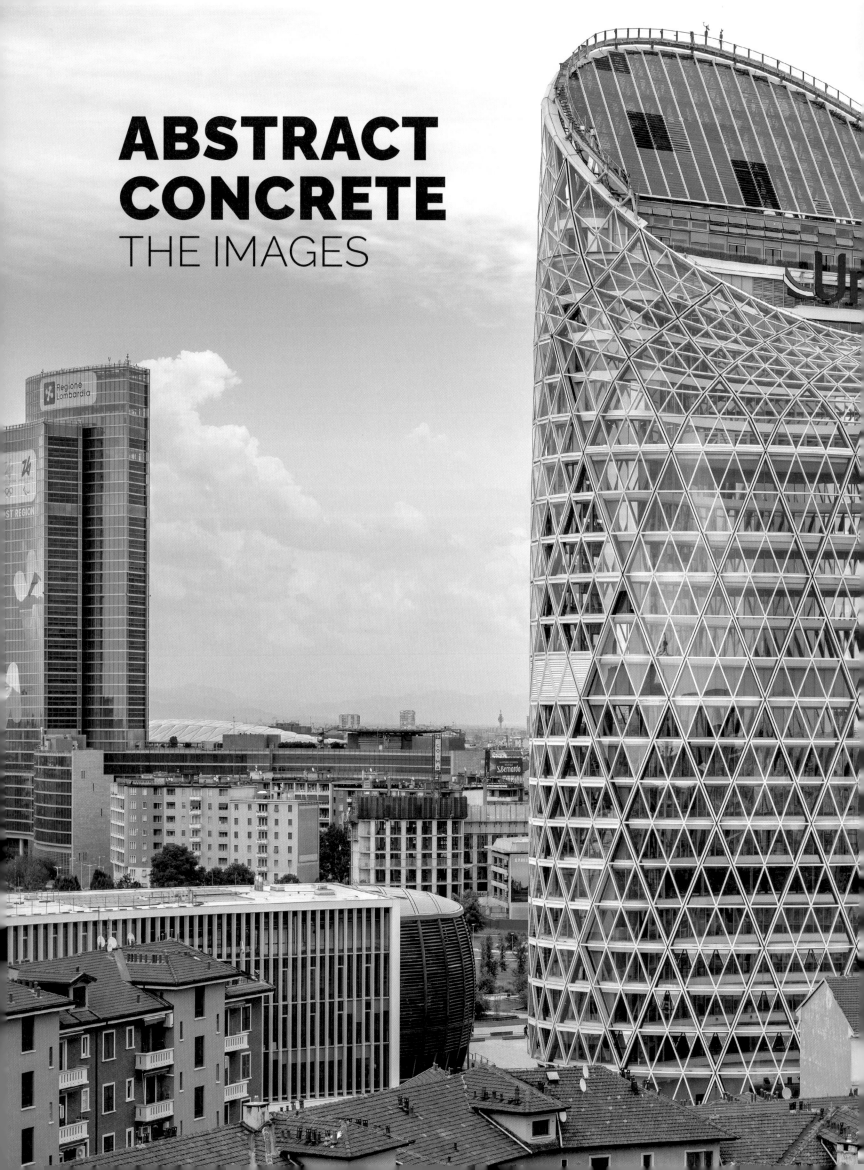

ABSTRACT CONCRETE
THE IMAGES

Here and previous pages
Works on the construction
of the base, which required
the creation of a foundation
pile system consisting
of 133 piles with a total length
of over 12,800 feet to support
the tower while spanning the
existing railway line below.

"WE WANTED TO CREATE A SYMBOL OF OUR ESSENCE THAT COULD EXPRESS A DISTINCTIVE LEADERSHIP IN THE ITALIAN FINANCIAL MARKET, ALSO BY MEANS OF THE LANGUAGE OF BEAUTY."

CARLO CIMBRI

The shape and visible details
of the diagrid have a significant
impact: they convey a satisfying
and even comforting sense
of the structure's dynamics.

The whole tower is clad
with 2,729 exterior glass panels.
The windows of the perimeter
offices feature quadruple
glazing with a layer of
intumescent magnetic coating.

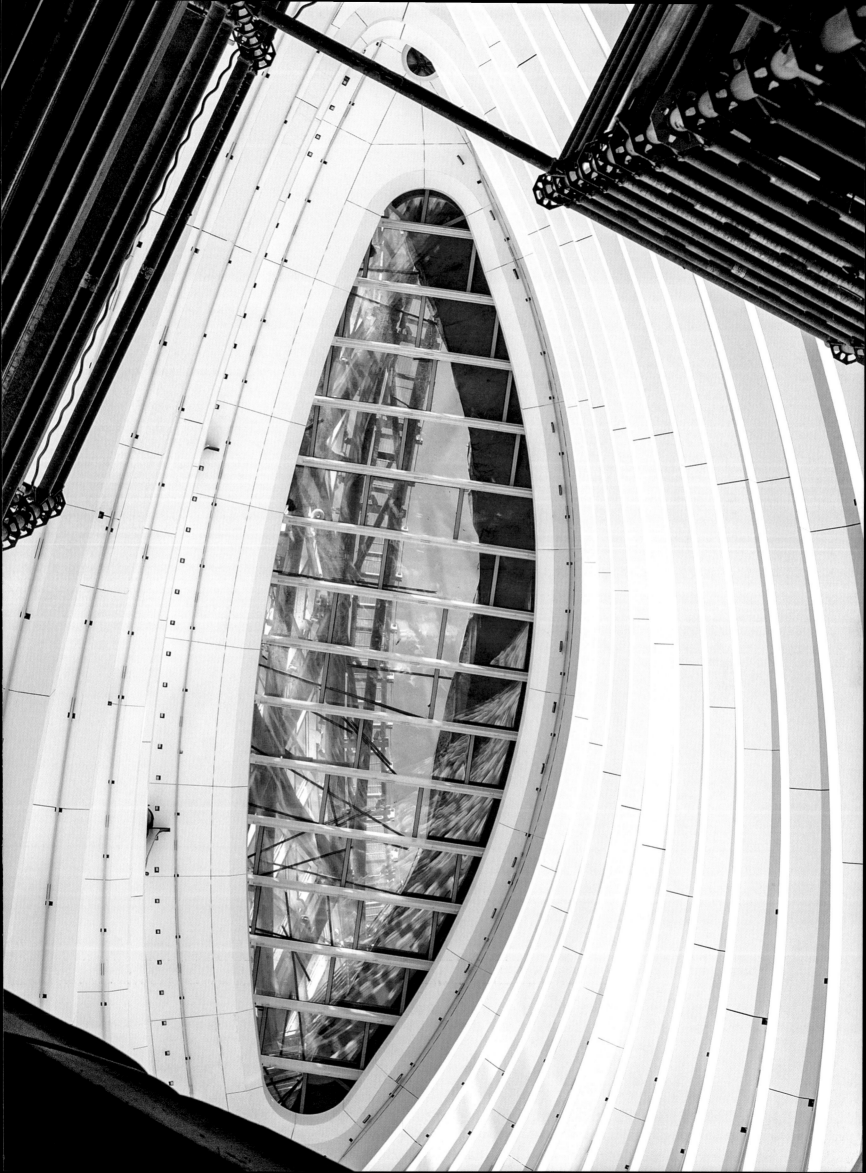

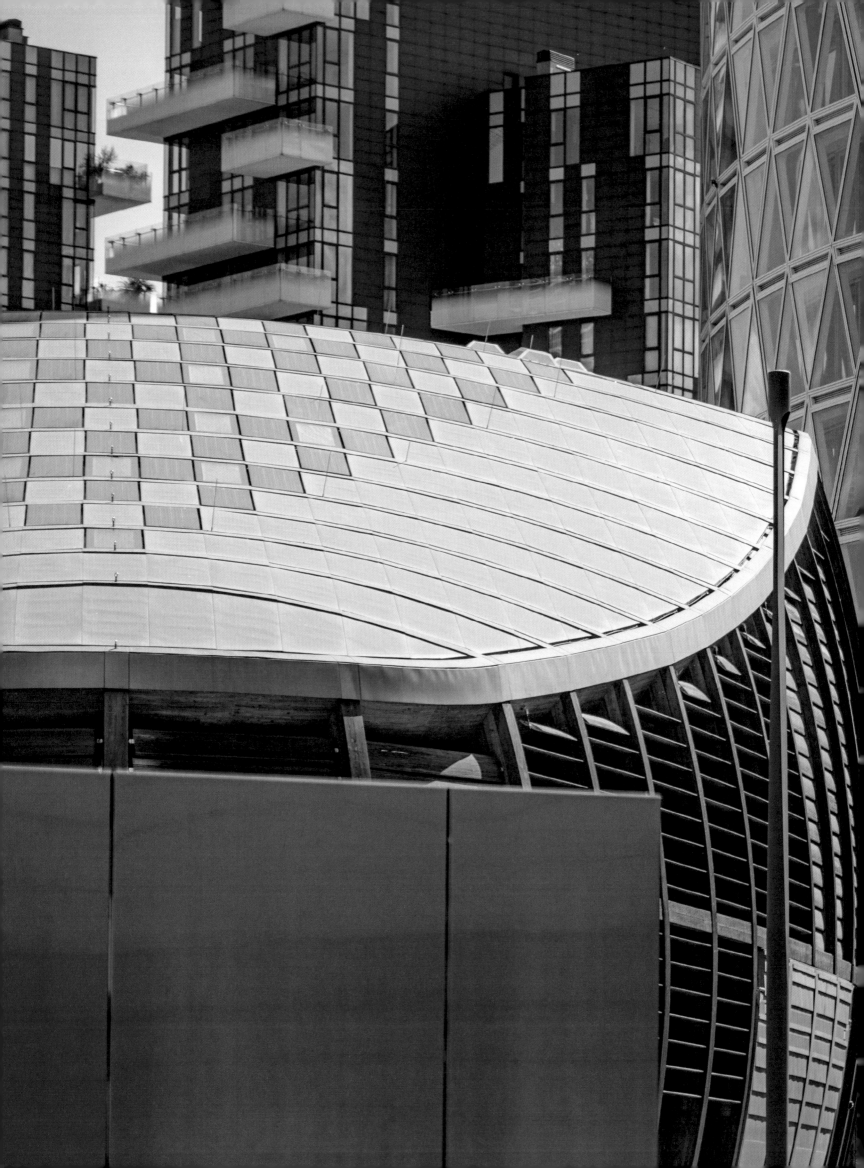

"WHILE WE USUALLY SOLELY USE THE STAIRWELL AS A LARGE SPINAL COLUMN SUPPORTING ALL THE FLOORS OF THE HIGH-RISE, THE UNIPOL TOWER ALSO RELIES PARTLY ON EXTERNAL LOAD-BEARING, INCREASING STATIC EFFICIENCY." **MASSIMO MAJOWIECKI**

"Due to its surrounding context, the Unipol Tower has a unique perceptual quality: there are points where it can only be seen in full from very close up and others only from a distance, a rather unusual situation for a skyscraper.

The building also has a false symmetry, in the sense that when you observe it closely, you perceive a continuous variation."
Duccio Malagamba, photographer

At the top, the tower is cut
at a 60-degree angle, creating
a covered plaza filled with
plants from the greenhouse
and served by a lounge.

"On the south side, the tower appears to passersby with its steel diagrid structure of intersecting lines enveloping the glass exterior and the cantilevered canopy at the entrance, which juts out 'like a piece of bark curled at the base of a tree trunk.'"
Mario Cucinella

Previous pages
The tower has a second raised
access on Piazza Gae Aulenti,
in addition to the one placed
below on the corner between
Via Melchiorre Gioia and
Via Fratelli Castiglioni.

Here and following pages
The canopy of the tower, designed to cover the entrance on Via Melchiorre Gioia, has become the focal point of a new square because of its unique shape, creating a truly urban landmark.

The "Unipol" sign establishes
the role of the new tower
on the Milanese skyline.

"THE INTEGRATION OF THE ATRIUM AND SQUARE DOES NOT JUST HAVE POSITIVE EFFECTS ON EXPANDING PUBLIC SPACE, ESPECIALLY IN A METROPOLITAN CONTEXT WHERE IT IS MOST NEEDED; IT HAS OTHER BENEFITS IN TERMS OF ENERGY AS WELL." **MARIO CUCINELLA**

"WE CAN SAY THAT OUR TOWER, THE UNIPOL TOWER – GROUP HEADQUARTERS MILAN, WAS NOT PURCHASED ON THE MARKET, BUT RATHER WAS BUILT BY US WITH OUR EFFORTS, DAY BY DAY, DETAIL BY DETAIL, ALONGSIDE ALL THE WORKERS, AND THERE ARE MANY, WHO CONSTRUCTED THE BUILDING." **CARLO CIMBRI**

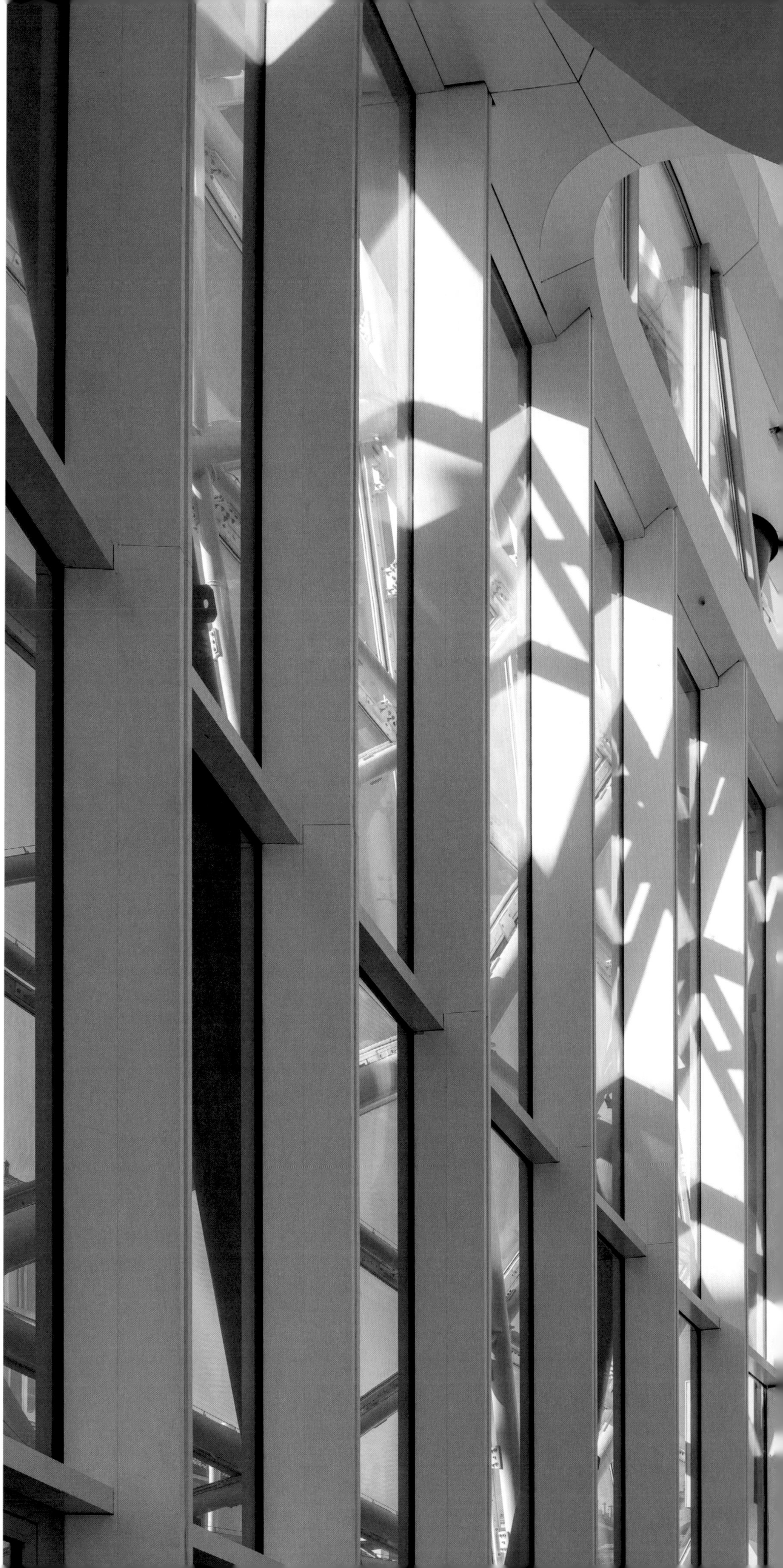

"Inside the tower, the visual experience is truly captivating: the light that penetrates from all sides changes continuously throughout the hours of the day or in the different seasons. I was particularly impressed by the intermediate floor, where one can overlook the grand hall, an extraordinary space that, in my opinion, embodies the exceptional nature of this architecture."
Duccio Malagamba

The large 18-story atrium
(over 230 feet high), which
occupies a third of the building's
total volume, represents the
physical and conceptual center
of the entire tower.

The offices overlooking the vast void of the central atrium, wrapping around it, allow one to fully grasp the building's vertical dimension.

Here and on the following pages
Some glimpses of the
workspaces: desks, break
areas, phone booths,
meeting rooms.

In these images and the
previous one, the meeting
rooms of an executive floor.

"In the case of the interior, the observer does not feel like they are inside an engineering structure; rather, it is like being in an enveloping space thanks to the all-encompassing presence of glass, that is, of light. In other words, the interior is more domestic, welcoming, and does not create a mechanical effect because it is pleasant and gentle."
Duccio Malagamba

The customized red staircase that connects the 19th to the 22nd floor is made of steel, with a powder-coated sheet metal finish and steps covered in serena stone.

The top level of the tower
houses the greenhouse,
a space where plants create
a large garden providing
a unique 360-degree view.

UNIPOL TOWER
BY THE NUMBERS

EXTERNAL WINDOWS AND GLASS

2,729

INTERNAL WINDOWS AND GLASS

1,886

WIDTH OF THE
CANTILEVERED CANOPY

62 feet

PILES USED

133

TOTAL LENGTH OF PILES USED

12,800 feet

PLANTS

3,279

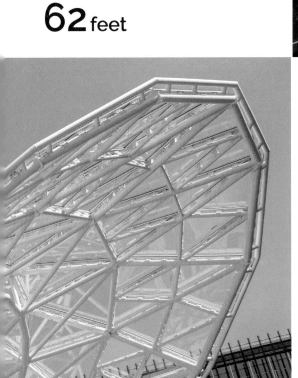

PEOPLE EMPLOYED

2,732

WELDING

8,500 feet

SOLAR PANELS

954

DIAGRID SEGMENTS

140

DIAGRID COLUMNS

293

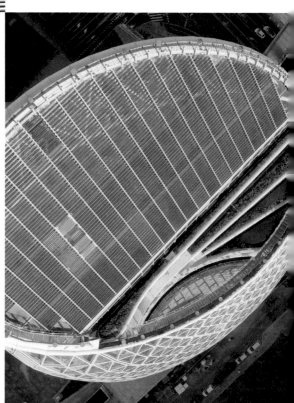

Photo Credits

© Duccio Malagamba: cover, pp. 1, 2–3, 4, 5, 6–7, 8, 9,
10–11, 12, 13, 14–15, 16, 20, 32–33, 46, 50–51, 66–67,
72, 74–75, 149, 150, 151, 152–53, 154, 155, 156–57, 158,
159, 160, 162, 163, 164, 165, 166, 167, 169, 170, 171, 172,
173, 174–75, 176–77, 178, 179, 180–81, 182–83, 184–85,
186, 187, 188–89, 191, 192, 193, 194, 195, 196, 198–99,
200, 201, 202, 204, 205, 206–207, 208–209, 210, 211,
212–13, 214, 215, 216–17, 218, 219, 220, 223, 224–25,
226, 227, 228–29

© Marco Garofalo: pp. 36–37, 38, 40, 43, 76, 77,
78–79, 80, 81, 82, 84–85, 86, 87, 88–89, 90, 92–93,
94–95, 97, 98, 99, 100–101, 102, 103, 104–105, 106–
107, 108–109, 110, 111, 112–13, 114, 115, 118–19, 120, 121,
122–23, 124, 125, 126–27, 128–29, 130–31, 132, 133, 134,
135, 136, 137, 138–39, 140–41, 230, 231 (except for
lower right)

© Nicola Bozzo and Fabrizio Bracco: pp. 26–27,
116-17, 142–43, 144–45, 146–47, 231 (lower right),
232–33, 234–35, 236, 238–39

Art Direction and Layout
Paola Ranzini Pallavicini

Translation by
Sylvia Adrian Notini

© 2024 Mondadori Libri S.p.A.
Distributed in English throughout the World by
Rizzoli International Publications, Inc.
49 West 27th Street
New York, NY 10001
www.rizzoliusa.com

ISBN: 978-88-918404-6-2

Printed in Italy
2025 2026 2027 2028 / 10 9 8 7 6 5 4 3 2 1

Visit us online:
Instagram.com/RizzoliBooks
Facebook.com/RizzoliNewYork
X: @Rizzoli_Books
Youtube.com/user/RizzoliNY